Celebrate
100 Days

Counting

Suzanne Barchers

Publishing Credits

Dona Herweck Rice, *Editor-in-Chief*; Lee Aucoin, *Creative Director*; Don Tran, *Print Production Manager;* Sara Johnson, *Senior Editor*; Jamey Acosta, *Assistant Editor;* Neri Garcia, *Interior Layout Designer;* Stephanie Reid, *Photo Editor*; Rachelle Cracchiolo, M.A.Ed., *Publisher*

Image Credits

cover Mike Flippo/Natelle/Shutterstock; p.1 Mike Flippo/Natelle/Shutterstock; p.4 Dmitriy Shironosov/Shutterstock; p.5 Kolja/Shutterstock; p.8 Monkey Business Images/Shutterstock; p.9 Beata Becla /Shutterstock; p.10 Fesus Robert/Shutterstock; p.11 Viktoria/Shutterstock; p.12 Vasina Natalia/Shutterstock; p.13 STILLFX/Ene/Shutterstock; p.14 Dainis/Shutterstock; p.15 Nataliya Hora/Shutterstock; p.16 Juan Jose Rodriguez Velandia/Shutterstock; p.17 Stephanie Reid; p.18 Emelyanov/Shutterstock; p.19 (left) Georgios Alexandris/Shutterstock, (right) Matthew Cole/Shutterstock; p.20 Monkey Business Images/Shutterstock; p.21 Rob Byron/Shutterstock; p.22 Feng Yu/Shutterstock; p.23 Cynthia Farmer/Shutterstock; p.24 Michael Chamberlin/Shutterstock; p.25 Samuel Acosta/Shutterstock; p.26 Terrie L. Zeller/Shutterstock; p.27 2happy/Shutterstock; p.28 3445128471/Shutterstock

Teacher Created Materials

5301 Oceanus Drive
Huntington Beach, CA 92649-1030
http://www.tcmpub.com
ISBN 978-1-4333-0415-6
©2011 Teacher Created Materials, Inc.
Printed in China
Nordica.072018.CA21800722

Table of Contents

The First Day of School 4

Counting to 100 6

Sets of 100 10

Things That Come in 100s 14

Finding Sets of 100 16

Measuring 100 18

Doing 100 Things 22

The 100th Day! 26

Solve the Problem 28

Glossary 30

Index 31

Answer Key 32

The First Day of School

Today is the first day of school. Our class makes big plans. We are planning for the 100th day of school.

We use the **calendar** to find the 100th day. Mr. Lin writes from 1 to 100 for each school day.

Hundred Board

1	2	3	4	5	6	7	8	9	10
11	12	13	14	15	16	17	18	19	20
21	22	23	24	25	26	27	28	29	30
31	32	33	34	35	36	37	38	39	40
41	42	43	44	45	46	47	48	49	50
51	52	53	54	55	56	57	58	59	60
61	62	63	64	65	66	67	68	69	70
71	72	73	74	75	76	77	78	79	80
81	82	83	84	85	86	87	88	89	90
91	92	93	94	95	96	97	98	99	100

LET'S EXPLORE MATH

When is your 100th day of school? Use your school calendar to find out.

Counting to 100

Our class learns something about 100 each month.

In September, we **count** to 100 a lot. We also write from 1 to 100. We write on big pieces of paper.

We list what we can count in a line. Some ideas are good. Some are silly.

Things to Line Up
100 shoes
100 cats
100 books
100 people
100 hats
100 blocks
100 clowns
100 monkeys
100 cookies
100 cups

4

6   7   8   9   10

We want to count 100 people. That is a lot of people! We line them up and count them.

11   12   13   14   15

Next we count books. Books do not move. They are easier to count in a line than people!

16 17 18 19 20

Sets of 100

In October, we make **sets** of 100. We make a list of the things we **collect**.

Things We Collect
rocks
toy cars
marbles
postcards
shells
stuffed bears
action figures
dolls
model airplanes
comic books

Ten students will bring in 10 of the same thing. That will make a set of 100. We vote on what to bring.

LET'S EXPLORE MATH

Look at the shells above. How many shells were brought into class?

We choose 10 students to bring in 10 rocks. They make 10 piles. Then, they put them in a bucket. It is heavy!

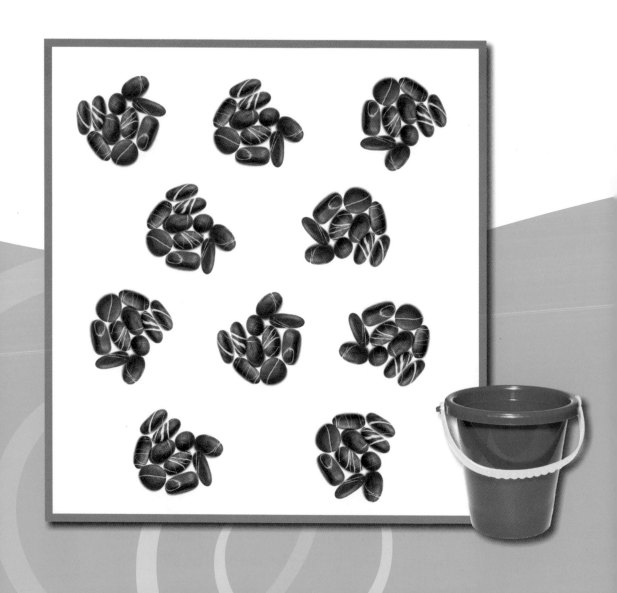

31   32   33   34   35

We choose 10 students to bring in 10 marbles. They make 10 piles. Then, they put them in a bucket. It is not as heavy as the rocks.

LET'S EXPLORE MATH

How many marbles are shown here?

36   37   38   39   40

Things That Come in 100s

November comes. We know a lot about 100 now. We want to find things that come in sets of 100.

41 **42** **43** **44** **45**

We start in our classroom. We make a list of all the things we find.

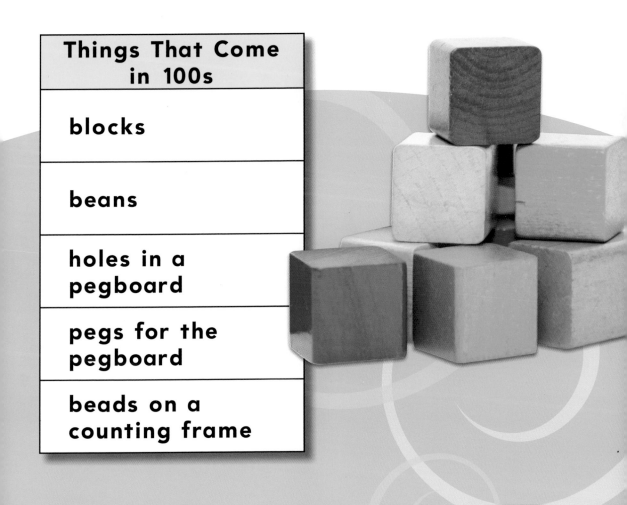

Things That Come in 100s
blocks
beans
holes in a pegboard
pegs for the pegboard
beads on a counting frame

46   47   48   49   50

Finding Sets of 100

In December, we look around our homes. We look for the number 100. We bring in what we find.

Some of us bring in the same things. Then, we make a **chart**. It shows how many of each package was found.

Sets of 100	
Item	**Number of Students Who Brought That Item**
	3
	4
	7
	5
	6

Measuring 100

Our class **measures** sets of 100 in January. We hook together 100 paper clips. The chain is very long.

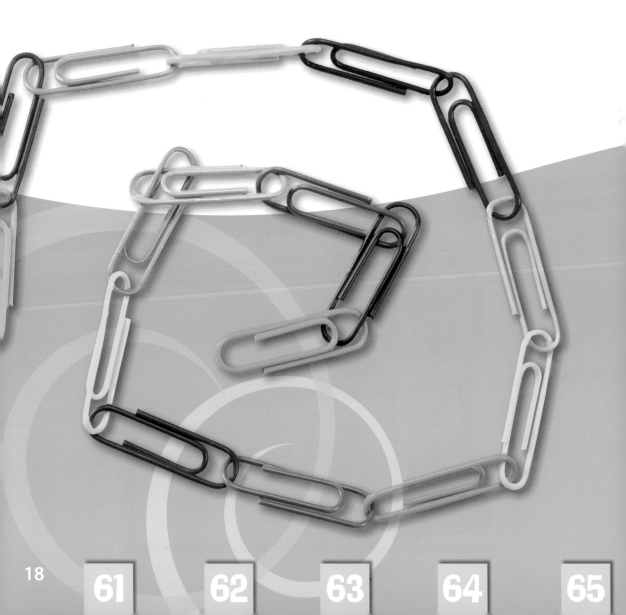

61 62 63 64 65

Next, we line up 100 toothpicks.
That line is even longer.

The students want to line up counters. First they have to count out 100 counters. Then they put the counters in groups of 10. Last they line up the counters.

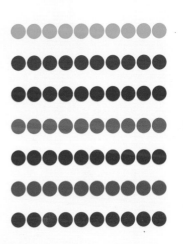

Look at the counters they have lined up so far.

a. How many counters are lined up?

b. How many more counters are needed to get to 100?

Next, we want to make a really long line. We **trace** around our feet. We cut out the paper feet. We have 50 feet. We make 50 more.

71   72   73   74   75

We put the 100 feet in a line down the hall. Our footprints go a long way!

76 77 78 79 80

Doing 100 Things

We list things we can do 100 times.

We can...
hop 100 times
read 100 books
eat 100 pieces of popcorn
go to school 100 days
make 100 cards
write 100 numbers
collect 100 things
learn 100 new things
measure 100 things
count 100 things

Mr. Lin asks us to do something new. It should use the number 100. It should be good for the school.

LET'S EXPLORE MATH

Mr. Lin's class wants to practice counting to 100 by doing something 100 times. Look at the list.

a. Name 2 activities that can be done quickly.

b. What would take the longest time to do?

We have a good idea. We pick up
100 pieces of trash at school.

91   **92**   **93**   **94**   **95**

It does not take long to pick up the trash. We have fun. The school looks great!

How Much Trash We Picked Up	
Type of Trash	**Number of Pieces**
paper	卌 卌 卌 卌
food wrappers	卌 卌
cans	卌 卌
water bottles	卌 卌 卌 卌
juice boxes	卌 卌 卌 卌
cups	卌 卌
straws	卌 卌

The 100th Day!

February 14th has come. It is the 100th day! We make 100 valentines. We give them to other students.

Then Mr. Lin has a surprise. It is a big cake. Guess how many candles are on it!

The picture below shows the number of candles Mr. Lin put on the cake. They are in groups of 10. How many candles were put on the cake?

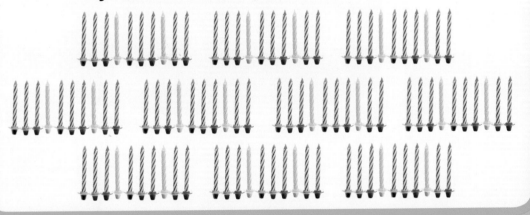

Counting Candles

A family is celebrating 2 big birthdays. Min is turning 10 years old. Mom is turning 40 years old. How many candles will they need for Min and Mom altogether?

Solve It!

Use the steps below to help you solve the problem.

Step 1: Min's cake needs 2 sets of 5.
Draw 2 sets of 5 like this.

Step 2: Draw sets of 5 for Mom's 40 candles.

Step 3: Count by 5s to get the total number
of candles.

Min's candles

||||| |||||

Mom's candles

||||| ||||| ||||| |||||

||||| ||||| ||||| |||||

Glossary

calendar—a chart of the days in each month of a year

chart—information that is put in columns and rows so that it is easy to read

collect—to gather things together

count—to add one by one in order to find the total number in a collection

measure—to find out what size something is

sets—groups of things

trace—to draw over lines or letters

Index

calendar, 5

chart, 17

collect, 10, 22

count, 6–9, 19, 22–23

line, 7–9, 19–21

list, 7, 10, 15, 22–23

marbles, 10, 13

measure, 18, 22

sets, 10, 14, 16–18

trace, 20

Let's Explore Math

Page 5:
Answers will vary.

Page 11:
100 shells

Page 13:
15 marbles

Page 19:
a. 70 counters
b. 30 more counters

Page 23:
a. Answers will vary but may include hopping 100 times, eating 100 pieces of popcorn, writing 100 numbers, and counting to 100.
b. going to school 100 days

Page 27:
100 candles

Solve the Problem

Min's candles

Mom's candles

They need 50 candles altogether.